Helping Children See Jesus

ISBN: 978-1-64104-005-1

The Tabernacle Part 1
A Picture of the Lord Jesus
Old Testament Volume 9:
Exodus Part 4

Author: Arlene Piepgrass and Katherine E. Hershey
Illustrator: Vernon Henkel
Computer Graphic Artist: Yuko Willoughby
Typesetting and Layout: Morgan Melton, Patricia Pope

© 2018 Bible Visuals International
PO Box 153, Akron, PA 17501-0153
Phone: (717) 859-1131
www.biblevisuals.org

All rights reserved. No part of this publication may be reproduced, stored in a retrieval system or transmitted in any form by any means, electronic, mechanical, photocopy, recording or otherwise, without the prior permission of the publisher, except as provided by USA copyright law.

RELATED ITEMS

To access related items (such as activities, memory verse posters and translated texts) please visit our web store at shop.biblevisuals.org and enter 2009 in the search box on the page.

FREE TEXT DOWNLOAD

To access a FREE printable copy of the teaching text (PDF format) in English or other available languages, enter S2009DL in the search box. Add the item to your cart, and use coupon code XTACSV17 at checkout. Once your order is processed you will receive an email with a link to the free download.

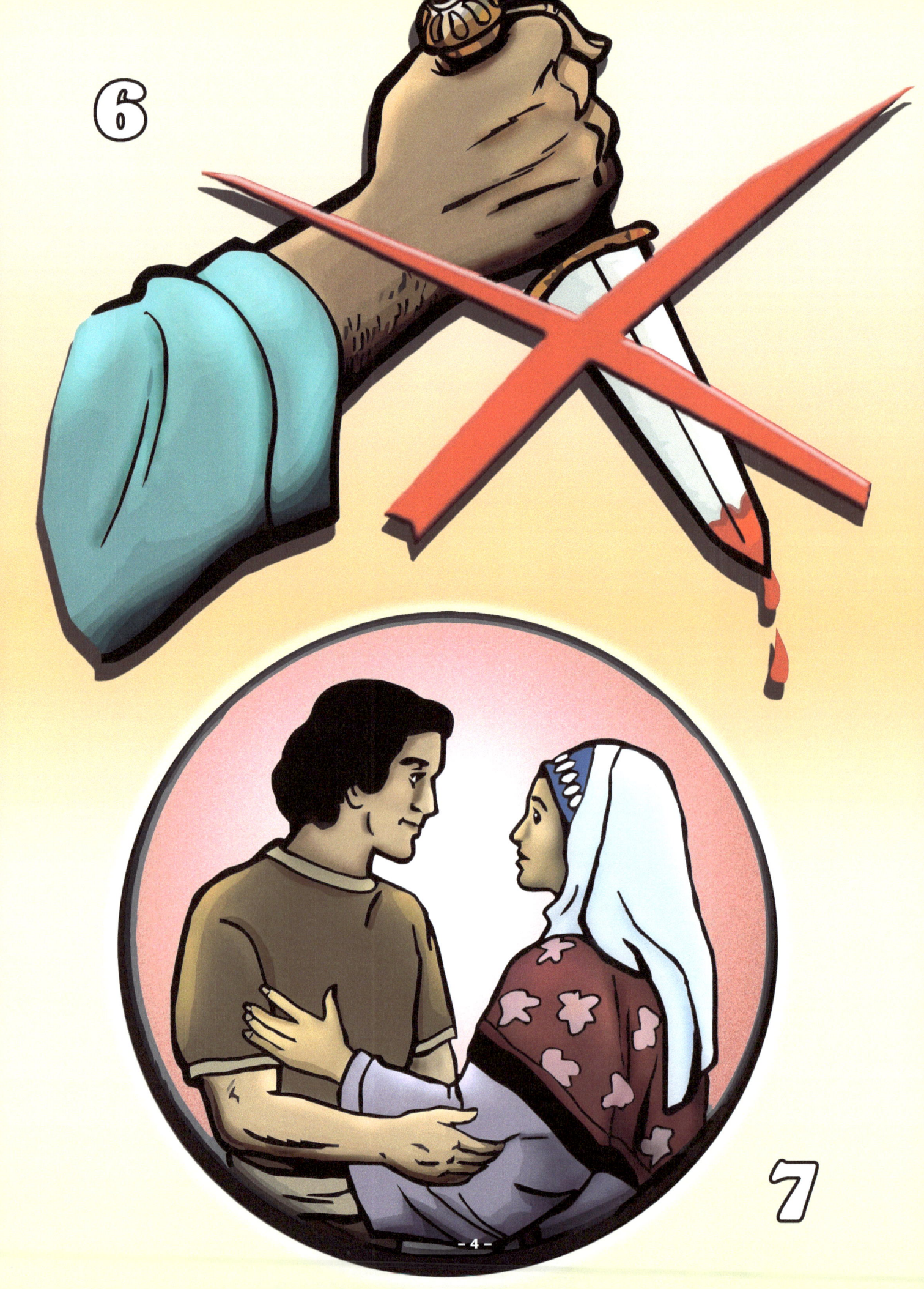

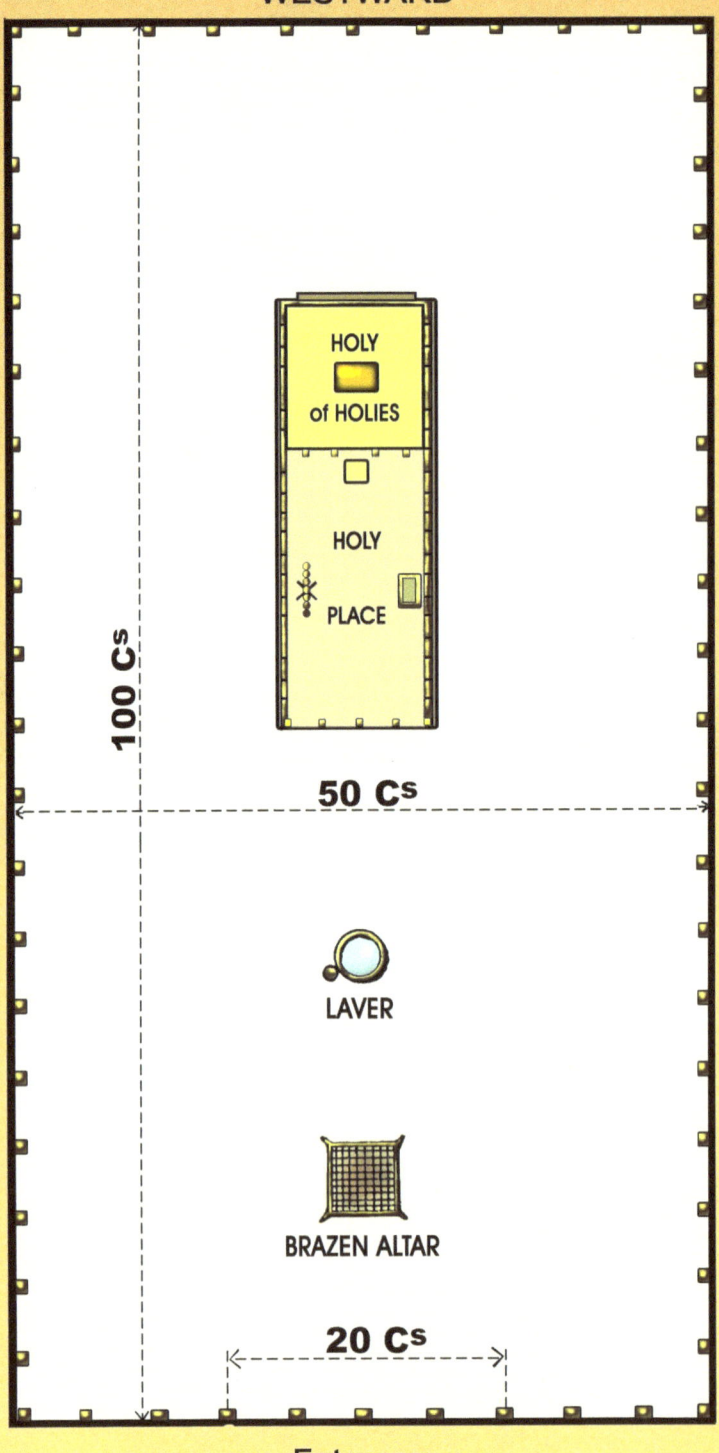

I am the door: by Me if any man enter in, he shall be saved.
John 10:9a

Unto Him that loved us, and washed us from our sins in His own blood.
Revelation 1:5b

© Bible Visuals International Inc

Lesson 1
GOD'S COMMANDS FOR HOLY LIVING

NOTE TO THE TEACHER

God gave the law to the Israelites: (1) to reveal His holiness; (2) to provide a standard of conduct; (3) to expose and identify sin. (See Romans 3:20; 7:7.) Today, Christian believers are not under the law given through Moses. (See Romans 6:14b.) "Christ is the end of the law for righteousness to everyone that believeth" (Romans 10:4). However this does not mean that the moral values of the Ten Commandments are discarded. Indeed, all–except the fourth commandment–are restated and enlarged upon in the teachings of the New Testament. (See Matthew 5:27-28; Ephesians 4:28; 6:1; Colossians 3:9; 1 John 5:21.)

We have stated each of the Ten Commandments briefly in two or three words. (See the ten laws in the first half of the lesson.) Your students should write these in their notebooks, and, if possible, memorize them. And if they are able to commit to memory the Ten Commandments in their entirety, fine!

Use illustrations 2 through 5 to teach the Ten Commandments and again when you show how they apply to us today. We have crossed out the idol (Illustration 2, #2) and the dagger (Illustration 4, #6) to indicate the thought that there are to be no idols and no murder.

Depending upon the ability of your group, it may be necessary to make two lessons out of this one. When teaching the latter part of the lesson, explain how each rule should affect your students; lives.

For your study we suggest that you refer to the entire text in New Testament Volume 27 and Volume 28, Lesson 4.

Scripture to be studied: Exodus 19–20; Deuteronomy 5

The *aim* of the lesson: To help your students understand that God's laws are for the good of His people.

What your students should *know*: The Holy Spirit will enable the child of God to obey the law of Christ.

What your students should *feel*: A desire to live according to the Word of God.

What your students should *do*: List in their notebooks any disobedience to God's Word. Determine how they can bring their lives into accord with God's rules.

Lesson outline for the teacher's and students' notebooks:
1. By obeying God, the Israelites would receive His blessings (Exodus 19:1-25).
2. God's laws for Israel's worship (Exodus 20:1-11).
3. God's law for Israel's family life (Exodus 20:12).
4. God's laws for Israel's daily living (Exodus 20:13-17).

The verse to be memorized:

He that hath My commandments and keepeth them . . . loveth Me. (John 14:21a)

THE LESSON

We live in a nation called _____. We are ruled by _____ (king, president, emperor, or chief) and other officials. These people make our laws and compel people to obey them. What are some of the laws in our country? (Let students discuss typical laws of your area.)

Why are laws needed? (*Teacher:* Encourage discussion.) Laws are guides for living. They help us to know what we may do and what we dare not do. They protect us. When everyone obeys the laws, living is easier and safer for all.

Even the best men in government are not perfect. So sometimes the laws they make are not good. But God says we must obey the laws of government–unless they are against His commands. (See Acts 5:29; Romans 13:1.)

1. BY OBEYING GOD, THE ISRAELITES WOULD RECEIVE HIS BLESSINGS
Exodus 19:1-25

When the people of Israel lived in Egypt, they obeyed the Egyptian laws. But God led the Israelites out of Egypt. After this, He alone was their Ruler.

In the wilderness one day, God called Moses to the top of the mountain. There He gave Moses instructions for the people. Moses listened carefully to everything God said.

Show Illustration #1

Going down the mountain, Moses gathered the Israelites together. "God has given me a message for you," he said. "Three months ago God led us out of Egypt. He opened the Red Sea so we could cross on dry ground. He destroyed the Egyptian army. He sent us food from Heaven. He has given us water in this wilderness. Now He wants to make a *covenant* (an agreement) with us. He wants us to be *His special nation.* He wants to *watch over us.* He wants to make us *successful* and give us *victory over our enemies.* Do you want these blessings?"

"Yes! Yes!" the people shouted eagerly.

"God has promised us all these good things if we will do what He says. He is our Ruler. He is holy. He is going to give us His laws. If we obey them, He will bless us."

"We will obey God's laws!" the people agreed heartily.

Three days later, they gathered near the mountain. They were eager to hear the laws. Suddenly there was the crack of thunder. Lightning flashed. A thick cloud covered the mountaintop. The trumpet of God blew loudly. The whole mountain appeared to be on fire as God came down upon it. The people were terrified.

God called Moses to the top of the mountain. There He gave these strict commands:

2. GOD'S LAWS FOR ISRAEL'S WORSHIP
Exodus 20:1-11

Show Illustration #2
Law #1: NO OTHER GODS

"I am the Lord your God. You shall have no other gods."

For more than 400 years the Israelites had lived in Egypt. There they saw the Egyptians worshiping all kinds of gods: the god of the river, the god of the sky, the god of the sun and many more. Alas, the

– 22 –

people of Israel began to worship false gods also! (See Joshua 24:14.)

Now God reminded them, "I am your God. You shall have no other gods."

Law #2: NO IDOLS

"Do not make idols . . . Do not worship them or serve them."

Idols are made by men. They may have eyes but they cannot see. Their ears cannot hear. Their lips cannot speak. (See Psalm 115:4-8; compare Isaiah 40:19; 44:14-19.)

To bow down to a god made of gold, wood or stone is to disobey God. He commanded, "Do not make idols or worship them."

Law #3: HONOR GOD'S NAME

"You shall not take the name of the Lord your God in vain."

To speak God's name without thought or meaning, is to use His name "in vain." Some people chant over and over again, "O God, God, God." Or, "O Lord, Lord, Lord." They hope to receive good things simply by saying God's name. Others use His name as a curse word. This, too, is to take God's name in vain. "Do not take the name of God in vain," God said.

Law #4: HONOR GOD'S DAY

*"Remember the Sabbath day, to keep it holy.
Six days you shall labor and do all your work."*

God wanted His people to be workers *and* worshipers. When He gave this command to the Jews, He told them to set apart the seventh day of the week (the Sabbath) as a day of worship. This reward of rest followed the duty of labor. They were not to do any kind of work on the Sabbath–not even light a fire! (See Exodus 35:2-3.) Anyone who disobeyed this law was to be put to death! As God had rested after six days of creation, so the Israelites were to rest after six days of work. (See Genesis 2:2.)

3. GOD'S LAW FOR ISRAEL'S FAMILY LIFE
Exodus 20:12

Law #5: HONOR PARENTS

"Honor your father and mother."

To honor parents is to respect and obey them.

Years after this command was given, the 12-year-old Jesus went with Mary and Joseph to Jerusalem. There they celebrated a Jewish feast (Passover). Afterwards His parents started home with the crowd. At the end of the day they discovered, to their amazement, that Jesus was not with the other young people.

Show Illustration #3

They hurried back to Jerusalem. There they found Him in the temple talking about God, His Father in Heaven. They insisted He had to leave the religious leaders and return with them. Jesus knew the Jewish law: "Honor your father and mother." And He obeyed Mary and Joseph.

4. GOD'S LAWS FOR ISRAEL'S DAILY LIVING
Exodus 20:3-17

Show Illustration #4

Law #6: NO MURDER

"You shall not murder."

Even before giving this law, God said, "He who murders another, shall be killed." (See Genesis 9:6.) Think of the seriousness of that! "You shall not murder."

Law #7: NO ADULTERY

"You shall not commit adultery."

Unmarried men and women are not to do together what they would do if they were married. Married couples are to live with each other until one dies. (See Genesis 2:24.) A man must never leave his wife for another woman. Neither may a woman leave her husband for some other man. To do so is to commit adultery. And God said, "You shall not commit adultery."

Show Illustration #5

Law #8: NO STEALING

"You shall not steal."

What is stealing? (Encourage student discussion. Include such things as failing to return something borrowed, wasting time at work, taking what belongs to others.) God insisted, "You shall not steal."

Law #9: NO LYING

"You shall not bear false witness against your neighbor."

To bear false witness is to lie. Have you ever known anyone to tell a lie? (Have class discuss the matter of lying.) God wanted His people to tell the truth always. "You shall not bear false witness," He commanded.

Law #10: NO COVETING

*"You shall not covet . . . anything that belongs to
your neighbor."*

Coveting is wanting for yourself what belongs to someone else. For example, you might want someone else's horse for yourself. That is coveting.

Sometimes breaking one command leads to breaking another. This can certainly be true of coveting. Some years after God gave these commandments, Ahab, a king of Israel coveted. Ahab owned many vineyards. Naboth, a farmer, had only one. King Ahab coveted Naboth's vineyard. He wanted it more than anything. But he could not have it.

Ahab pouted. He even refused to eat! His wicked wife said, "Do not worry, Ahab. I shall get the vineyard for you." And she went to work at once.

First, she hired men *to tell lies* about Naboth. As a result, the people dragged Naboth outside the city and *stoned him to death*. Then she told her husband to *take the vineyard*.

Ahab began by breaking commandment #10. Before getting what he wanted, which other commands were broken? *(Numbers 6, 8, 9)*

"You shall not covet," was God's tenth command.

More than 3,000 years have passed since God gave these laws (and more than 600 others!) to the Jewish people. They were holy commands and good. (See Romans 7:12.) But they were rigid and unbending. To receive God's blessing, the people *had* to obey all the laws (See Exodus 19:5-8.). To disobey a command was sin. (See Deuteronomy 27:26; Galatians 3:10.) And sin had to be punished.

When Christ–the perfect One–died, He took the punishment for all sin. Today, instead of living according to the law given through Moses, we live by another law: "the law of Christ". (See Galatians 6:2; compare James 1:25; Romans 8:2.) Instead of obeying the old law *in order to get blessed,* we are to obey the new law *because we have been blessed*. We obey because we *want* to, not because we *have* to. Certain rules in the law of Christ are much like those given to the Israelites long ago.

For example:

#1 "You shall love the Lord your God with all your heart, with all your soul and with all your mind." (See Matthew 22:37.)

Is there anything or anyone you love more than God? If so, that person or that thing has become your god. But you are to *love God with all your heart*!

#2 "Flee from idolatry" (1 Corinthians 10:14; compare Galatians 5:20).

To pray to an idol is to disobey God. If you are sick, to whom do you go for help? Do you go to the doctor's mother? Or to a friend of your doctor? No! You go to the doctor himself. Just so, God commands you to pray directly to Him. *No idols!*

#3 "Honor God's name, for it is holy." (See Matthew 6:9; compare Psalm 111:9.)

The Lord Jesus commanded His disciples: "When you pray, do not use vain repetitions, as the pagans do. They think they will be heard for their much speaking. Do not be like them." (See Matthew 6:7-8.) Then He taught them how they *should* pray. He began: "Our Father in Heaven, Your name is holy."

You must *never* use God's name carelessly. You are always to speak of Him with respect and honor. *Honor God's holy name.*

#4 The Lord's Day

Nine of the Ten Commandments are repeated in the New Testament. The one which begins, "Remember the Sabbath day" is *not* mentioned. Here is the reason. The Lord Jesus Christ rose from the dead on the first day of the week. Ever since, His people have worshiped and served Him on the first day of the week. It is the Lord's Day–the day of resurrection (See Matthew 28:1-6; 1 Corinthians 16:2; Revelation 1:10.). Do you *honor the Lord on His day?*

#5 "Honor your parents." (See Ephesians 6:1-3.)

To please the Lord, children must obey their Christian parents. (See Colossians 3:20.) Old and young alike are always to *honor* their parents. Do you *honor your mother and father*?

#6 "Whoever hates his brother is a murderer." (See 1 John 3:15; compare Matthew 5:21-22; Romans 13:9.)

The commandments God gave to His people, the Israelites, were strict. The law of Christ is even more severe. For He says that *anyone who even hates his brother is a murderer!*

#7 "Looking at a woman with a sinful desire of wanting her, is to commit adultery in the heart." (See Matthew 5:27-28.)

What you *look* at and what you *think* can be as sinful as what you *do*, Christ warned. *Do not commit adultery.*

#8 "Do not steal. Work so you can have what you need and give to those who need help." (See Ephesians 4:28.)

Remember! God is watching you all the time wherever you are. (See Psalm 139:7-12; Jeremiah 23:24.) He has promised to supply all your need. (See Philippians 4:19.) His "supply" may include whatever work you must do to earn what you need. *Do not steal!*

#9 "Speak the truth . . ." (See Ephesians 4:25, Colossians 3:9.)

Ask the Lord every day to set a watch over your mouth and keep the door of your lips. (See Psalm 141:3.) He is the only One who can help you to *tell the truth always*.

#10 "Be content with what you have." (Hebrews 13:5; compare Ephesians 5:5.)

If you are truly content with what you have, you will not covet what belongs to others. *Put to death covetousness, which is idolatry.* (See Colossians 3:5.)

The law of Christ contains hundreds of specific rules. Some are commands to do certain things. Others tell us what not to do. All the rules are perfect. If we are going to obey them, we must have more power than we ourselves have. Happily, God who gave the law of Christ, has also provided the power to obey His commands. That power is the Holy Spirit who lives within each Christian from the moment he is born again. (See John 14:17; Romans 8:9; 1 Corinthians 6:19.)

God has doubtless spoken to you today of some command, some rule you have not been obeying. Now you want to obey Him. Will you write that command in your notebook? Then together we shall ask Him to help you to obey Him gladly.

Lesson 2
GOD FORBIDS IDOLATRY

NOTE TO THE TEACHER

People tend to think of God as being like themselves (Psalm 50:21). They change His glory into images that look like men, or birds, beasts or creeping things. (See Romans 1:21, 23.) This is idolatry. And idolatry is sin. (See Exodus 20:2-3; 1 John 5:21; 1 Corinthians 10:7, 14.) God says, "I am the Lord: that is My name: and My glory will I not give to another, neither My praise to graven images" (Isaiah 42:8). God hates idolatry.

God's wrath against sin is as much a part of His nature as is His love for the sinner. (See Deuteronomy 9:19-20; Psalm 7:11; Romans 1:18.)

Pray for yourself, teacher, that you may understand God's holiness, majesty and power. Pray that your students may learn that He *will* not share His glory with another. Help them to see the exceeding holiness of God and the awful sinfulness of idolatry.

Scripture to be studied: Exodus 32:1–34:35; Deuteronomy 9:8-21; Acts 7:38-41

The *aim* of the lesson: To show that God will not share His glory, honor, or worship with anyone or anything. (See Isaiah 44:6.)

What your students should *know*: Idols are an insult to God's greatness, glory and power.

What your students should *feel*: A hatred for worshiping anything or anyone other than God.

What your students sho*uld do*: Get rid of all idols which have come between them and God.

Lesson outline for the teacher's and students' notebooks:

1. Idolatry of the people (Exodus 32:1-6).
2. God's people dare not worship false gods (Exodus 32:7-10).
3. Moses prays for the sinful Israelites (Exodus 32:11-35).
4. God again gives His promises to His people (Exodus 33:14–34:28).

The verse to be memorized:

He that hath My commandments and keepeth them . . . loveth Me. (John 14:21a)

THE LESSON

Children are able to learn what their parents want them to do or not to do. Students in school can usually understand all the school rules. But is it just as easy to *obey* all the rules at school or in the home? Do people always obey what they know?

Moses gave God's laws to the people. Immediately they agreed, "All that the Lord has said, we will do and be obedient" (Exodus 24:7).

So God told Moses, "Come to the top of the mountain again. I have more instructions for My people."

Turning to the Israelites, Moses ordered, "You wait down here for me. My brother Aaron will help you while I am gone."

The Israelites watched Moses go up the mountain. The mountaintop appeared to be on fire. But it did not burn. For the glow was really the shining glory of God. Moses disappeared right up into the cloud of fire to listen to God.

"Moses," God began, "I want you to make a Tabernacle (a movable tent). I will meet with you in the Tabernacle. There I will talk with you."

Moses stayed on the mountaintop forty days and forty nights. God told him exactly how to build the Tabernacle and all that was to go in it.

1. IDOLATRY OF THE PEOPLE
Exodus 32:1-6

As Moses was listening to God, the people below could not see him. They could not hear God's voice. Life went on as usual down in the camp. Almost six weeks went by. Moses did not return. The people became restless. They had many questions: "What happened to Moses?" "Did he get lost or have an accident?" "Could he have been destroyed by the fire?"

Going to Aaron, they said, "We do not know what has become of Moses. He led us out of Egypt. But now he has disappeared. Make us a god to lead us. We want a god we can see!"

Aaron should have been horrified. He should have insisted, "No, no! We do not need a god to lead us. We do not need an idol to take the place of the living God of Heaven. Six weeks ago you promised God that you would not make idols nor bow down to them. God will punish you if you do!"

Show Illustration #6

But, alas, Aaron said no such thing. Indeed, he completely ignored the law of God. He ordered the people to bring all their golden earrings to him. Melting the gold, Aaron shaped it into a calf.

When the people saw the calf, they were delighted. They shouted, "O Israel, this is the god which brought us out of Egypt!"

When Aaron saw how happy they were, he built an altar in front of the golden calf. He announced, "Tomorrow we shall have a feast to the Lord!"

2. GOD'S PEOPLE DARE NOT WORSHIP FALSE GODS
Exodus 32:7-10

Show Illustration #7

The next day, deliberately disobeying God's law, the people offered sacrifices to their idol. They ate and drank and danced.

How could they have forgotten God so quickly? (How quickly do *you* forget what you learn about Him? Do you ever shut Him out of your life?)

We like to think that God is loving. And He is. But the Bible also tells us that "God is angry with the wicked every day." (See Psalm 7:11.) Because God is holy and just, He must and will punish those who disobey His holy Word. (See Revelation 6:17; Luke 12:5; Romans 2:8.)

Just six weeks before, God had commanded the Israelites, "you shall have no other gods but Me. I the Lord your God am jealous. If you disobey Me, you will be punished." (See Exodus 20:3, 5.)

God was angry when He saw His people deliberately turn from Him to an idol. So He said to Moses, "How quickly your people have forgotten My commandments! They are stubborn and rebellious. They have not kept their part of the covenant (agreement). I am going to kill all of them. Do not try to stop Me, Moses."

3. MOSES PRAYS FOR THE SINFUL ISRAELITES
Exodus 32:11-35

Show Illustration #8

"O God," Moses pleaded earnestly, "do not destroy these people. You redeemed them from Egypt. I know they deserve Your anger and Your judgment. But the Egyptians will think you brought them to the wilderness to kill them. You promised to lead them to the land of Canaan. Oh, do not kill them!" Moses begged.

With great mercy, God answered, "I have heard your prayer, Moses. I will not destroy My people, the Israelites."

Then Moses went down the mountain. Carefully he carried the two stone tablets on which God had written the Ten Commandments. When he got close to the camp, he saw with his own eyes the people worshipping the golden calf. He became so furious that he hurled the tablets to the ground, breaking them into pieces.

He pitched the calf into the fire, melted it and ground it into powder. Then he poured it over the water and made the people drink it.

"You have broken your agreement with God!" he shouted. "You have turned your backs on the living and powerful One. You have chosen to worship an idol–an idol that could never do anything for you! God will not allow this! All of you who are on the Lord's side, come over here and join me," Moses commanded.

Immediately all the men of the tribe of Levi went to stand with Moses. They believed God was right. They knew it was wrong to worship the golden calf.

Moses ordered, "You men of Levi, take your swords. God has commanded that you go through the camp and kill those who have led in this awful sin."

The Levites obeyed at once. And three thousand men were

killed that day. Death was God's punishment for sin. It still is! (See Ezekiel 18:4b; Romans 6:23.)

That night, in their tents, the remaining people had great fear. *What will happen now?* they wondered. *Will God forgive us? Shall we all die?*

The next day Moses gathered the people together. "You have sinned wickedly," he said. "But I shall ask God to forgive you."

With unusual earnestness, Moses prayed, "O God, these people have sinned a great sin. In making a god of gold, they have done what You have forbidden. They do not deserve Your mercy, O God. But will You please forgive them? If not, let me die for them, I pray."

God answered, "No, Moses, you cannot die for them. Each one must die for his own sins. But I have heard your prayer. Go to the people and lead them to the land of which I told you. Because they are stubborn and rebellious I shall not go with them. Instead, I shall send My Angel to go before you."

"O God," Moses begged, "You have said I have found favor in Your sight. If this is true, do not ask me to lead these people without Your presence!"

4. GOD AGAIN GIVES HIS PROMISES TO HIS PEOPLE
Exodus 33:14–34:28

"Moses, you have found favor in My sight. You are My friend. I have heard your prayer. I will go with you," God promised.

God continued, "Come up to the mountaintop in the morning. Come alone. Bring two new stone tablets."

Show Illustration #9

Moses made two tablets of stone like the first ones. He arose early in the morning and, taking the tablets, climbed the mountain. The Lord came down in the cloud. Immediately Moses bowed, worshiped and prayed, "O Lord, forgive our sin. Accept us as Your special people." (See Exodus 34:9.)

God promised, "I shall renew My covenant with My people. I shall do miracles such as have never before been done in all the earth. All the people of Israel shall see My power–the power I shall display through you, Moses. If you will obey all of My commandments, I shall chase all your enemies out of the land which I am giving you. You must never make any agreements with those enemies. You must destroy all their false gods, their images and altars. You must not worship any other god but Me. You must be absolutely loyal to Me . . . You must have nothing to do with idols."

This all happened more than 3,000 years ago. But the Word of God has not changed. God hates idolatry today exactly as He did in the time of Moses. He warns us, "Do not be idolators as were some of the Israelites . . . flee from idolatry!" (See 1 Corinthians 10:7, 14.)

Anything that comes between you and God, anything more important to you than God, is an idol. He says, "I am the Lord; that is My name: and My glory shall I not give to another . . ." (See Isaiah 42:8.) "Little children, keep yourselves from idols" (1 John 5:21).

Think carefully now. Is there something or someone which has come between you and God? Is there anything more important to you than God? It may be very precious. It may be something important. Perhaps it is money. Maybe it is pleasure. It could be your work. Or it may be a friendship. Whatever you crave on earth more than the true and living God is an idol. And God hates idolatry.

List in your notebook any idol that you have. Then together let us ask God for courage to get rid of that idol right now. Mention also in your notebook what you plan to do this week when you are tempted to return to your idol.

Lesson 3
THE WAY OF APPROACH TO GOD

NOTE TO THE TEACHER

This lesson and the next, together with those in Volume Ten, are a study of Tabernacle typology. "A type is a divinely purposed illustration of some truth. It may be: (1) a person (Romans 5:14); (2) an event (1 Corinthians 10:11); (3) a thing (Hebrews 10:19-20); (4) an institution (Hebrews 9:11-12) or (5) a ceremonial (1 Corinthians 5:7). Types occur most frequently in the first five books of the Bible. But they are found, more sparingly, elsewhere" (Note from the *New Scofield Bible*).

Strictly speaking, a type is that which has been so indicated in the Bible. In our earlier study of Joseph (see Volumes Four and Five of this series), we saw many *likenesses* between him and the Lord Jesus Christ. But the Bible does not speak of him as a type of Christ. However the Tabernacle is mentioned as a type (Other Bible words for "type" are: *ensample* (1 Corinthians 10:11); *example* (Hebrews 8:5); *figure* (Romans 5:14); *pattern* (Titus 2:7); *print* (John 20:25).).

The Tabernacle has three meanings. (1) It is a type–a visible illustration–of God's heavenly dwelling (Hebrews 9:23-24). (2) It is a type of the Lord Jesus Christ who is the meeting place between God and man (John 14:6; 1 Timothy 2:5). (3) It is a type of Christ in the Church–of the communion of Jesus with all believers (Revelation 21:3).

Your students must see clearly the *purpose* of the Tabernacle. The Lord Himself said, "And let them make Me a sanctuary; that I may dwell among them" (Exodus 25:8). The days of their Egyptian slavery were over. Now they were traveling through the dreary wilderness to the land God had promised them. And God yearned for communion and fellowship with His people.

From the very beginning, the Lord God has always wanted to be with His people. He walked and talked with Adam and Eve at the close of each day–until they sinned and spoiled it all. He dwelt among His people in the Tabernacle. Hundreds of years later our blessed Lord became flesh and dwelt (tabernacled) among men. (See John 1:14.) God longed continually to dwell with His people to have instant and constant fellowship with them. After the Lord Jesus finished His atoning work, He returned to the Father. Then the Holy Spirit came to dwell within believers. (See John 14:16-17; 16:13.) God, the holy One, could have withdrawn from the sinful Israelites. He could have turned His back upon us. Instead, He chose always to be with His people where they are. Oh, what love!

We have sought to simplify the tremendous truths of the Tabernacle by teaching the lessons in story form.

Scripture to be studied: Exodus 34:28-35; 27:9-18; 35:4–36:7; 38:9-18

The *aim* of the lesson: To show that, although man's sinfulness separates him from God's holiness, God has made a way of reconciliation through Christ.

What your students should *know*: That God is perfectly holy, but man is utterly sinful.

What your students should *feel*: A sense of their own sinfulness and separation from God.

What your students should *do*: Come to God through Christ for salvation.

Lesson outline for the teacher's and students' notebooks:

1. Moses returns to the camp (Exodus 34:28-35).
2. Moses and his message (Exodus 35:4-19).
3. Response of the people (Exodus 35:20–36:7).
4. The court and the gate (Exodus 27:9-18; 38:9-18).

The verse to be memorized:

I am the door: by Me if any man enter in, he shall be saved. (John 10:9a)

THE LESSON
1. MOSES RETURNS TO THE CAMP
Exodus 34:28-35

Show Illustration #10

Phinehas stood near the Sinai mountain in the camp of the Israelites. "Father, when will Uncle Moses come down from the mountain?" he asked.

"I do not know, my son," Eleazar answered soberly. "Forty days is a long, long time for him to be gone."

"Grandfather Aaron will not make another golden calf, will he, Father?" Phinehas asked.

"No, Phinehas, I am sure your grandfather will not make another golden calf."

Both father and son remembered with sadness the wicked idol-making the last time Moses had been on the mountaintop.

We are not exactly certain how old Phinehas was when the children of Israel camped at Mount Sinai. The Bible mentions him several times. (See Exodus 6:25; Numbers 25:7; 31:6; Joshua 22:13-32; Judges 20:28.) But it does not tell of his boyhood. We do know that, as a boy, Phinehas camped with the Israelites. He doubtless knew more than many other boys about God's dealings with His people. For Phinehas was the grandson of Aaron, and the grandnephew of Moses.

In our next few lessons you will learn many interesting facts, as Phinehas learned them. When you read your Bible, however, you will not find Phinehas asking questions. We actually don't know what he asked. But boys the age of Phinehas have many questions. They want to learn all they possibly can. Although Phinehas lived long ago, he was much the same as any boy today. So we are going to think of the things which may have happened when he was a boy.

2. MOSES AND HIS MESSAGE
Exodus 35:4-19

"Look, Phinehas!" his father exclaimed. "Here comes Uncle Moses now!"

Show Illustration #11

"How strange his face looks! It is so bright it hurts to look at him." Phinehas squinted his eyes as Moses came nearer.

Eleazar blinked. Others, too, saw the same brightness. "What makes Moses' face shine like that?" everyone wanted to know. And they were afraid!

"Come closer," Moses called. Slowly Aaron and the leaders moved toward him.

Phinehas whispered, "He doesn't even know his face is shining."

It was true. Moses did *not* know his face shone–not until someone told him. So he covered his face with a veil. Then the people were not afraid when he spoke to them.

"This is the thing the Lord commanded," Moses began. Phinehas listened carefully. God's commands were important. "Whoever is of a willing heart, let him bring an offering to the Lord."

An offering? What kind of offering?

Carefully the people listened as Moses told them what God wanted. "The Lord needs gold, silver and bronze; blue, purple and scarlet and fine linen. He needs goats' hair, rams' skins dyed red, and badger skins. He wants acacia wood, oil, spices and incense and precious stones."

Phinehas's eyes grew big. What a lot of different things! *How can the Lord use all these things?* he wondered.

Moses continued, "The Lord has commanded that we make a Tabernacle for Him. It is to be a movable tent. God will meet with us, His people, at the Tabernacle. The Lord gave me the pattern for this up on the mountain."

3. RESPONSE OF THE PEOPLE
Exodus 35:20–36:7

Show Illustration #12

Almost as soon as Moses finished speaking, the people began bringing their gifts to the Lord. Phinehas wondered where everything came from. The wood, he knew, was from the trees near the mountain. The animals, too, were from the mountain area. They would be killed and their skins taken off. But gold, silver, precious stones! Where could the people ever get such gifts? Then Phinehas remembered! Before they came into this wilderness, the Egyptians had given them these very things. God had commanded the Israelites to ask the Egyptians for them. The Jewish people had not been paid when they were forced to work as slaves in Egypt. The gold and silver and gems were really like back wages.

Now the people were bringing them to Moses. All that day they brought their offerings. And the next day. And the next. Moses had said, "Everyone of a willing heart" was to bring an offering. And every man, every woman, every boy, every girl, had a willing heart!

Phinehas's mother worked with some of the other women. They spun fine linen and beautiful cloth of blue and purple and scarlet. This was their offering.

Phinehas wanted to bring something too. He had a little silver trinket–a gift from a friend in Egypt. He had meant to keep it to remember his friend. But something inside Phinehas made him want to give it to the Lord. So when the other people brought their offerings, Phinehas brought his, too. How happy he was to know that God would use his gift!

Then Moses spoke again. "The Lord has called Bezaleel to oversee the work of building the Tabernacle. Aholiab will be his assistant. God has given them special wisdom to work with gold and silver and bronze in cutting stones, and in woodworking."

Bezaleel and Aholiab chose many workmen to help build the unusual and wonderful tent.

As the people brought their offerings, the work progressed. Goldsmiths and silversmiths melted the bracelets, earrings and rings. They molded them to fit in the right places in the Tabernacle.

Finally one day the workmen told Moses, "Tell the people to stop bringing their offerings. We have more than enough to finish the Tabernacle." So Moses sent word to all the people, "Do not bring any more gifts."

Phinehas watched the workmen closely day by day. There were many things he and other boys and girls could do. There were errands to run. There were messages to be carried.

4. THE COURT AND THE GATE
Exodus 27:9-18; 38:9-18

Show Illustration #13

A day came when men hung big linen curtains in place. The curtains were seven and one-half feet from top to bottom. (*Teacher:* Compare to height of your room.) Phinehas observed that even the tallest man could not see over the top. The curtains were hung close together on silver pillars. The curtains measured 150 feet long on each side and 75 feet at each end. (*Teacher:* Use comparisons. For example, "As far as from here to the street and from our house to the house next door.") On the south, west and north the curtains were solid white with no opening. On the east side, there was a wide gate. The hanging at the gate was made of blue, purple and scarlet woven into fine linen.

Phinehas soon learned that the curtain fence enclosed the "court." (You will want to remember that. Let's say it together: "The court.")

"Father, please tell me about the curtain," Phinehas begged.

"The curtains are white, my son, to remind us of God's righteousness and holiness. God can have no contact with sin. The white tells of that purity which belongs to God alone."

"Why are the curtains so high and so close together?" Phinehas wanted to know.

Eleazar explained, "There is no way man can come to God. No way *over*. No way *under*. No way *through*. God is holy. And we are oh, so sinful! However, there is one way of entrance."

Phinehas saw his father look at the beautiful curtain hanging at the east gate. Eleazar explained even before Phinehas asked about it. "The blue is a heavenly color. The purple is a royal color, one worn by kings. And scarlet is the color of sacrifice."

Phinehas could *not* know some of the wonderful things we know. He lived many years before the Lord Jesus lived. He knew only that God would someday send a Saviour. Today we know the words of the Saviour, "I am the door: by Me if any man enter in, he shall be saved." And, "I am the way, the truth and the life. No one comes to the Father, but by Me." (See John 10:9; 14:6.) The Lord Jesus is the *only* way to God.

God is holy and we are sinful. There is no way *through* to God except one. (See John 3:3.) There is no way *around*–you cannot find another door anywhere. There is no way *under* the curtains. There is no way *over* the curtains. We cannot work our way to God. But the Lord Jesus Christ is waiting for us to come to God through Himself.

God's Tabernacle is a lovely picture of the Lord Jesus Christ in many different ways. This is why the pattern God gave was so exact. It had to be an absolutely perfect picture of the perfect Son of God. The blue in the curtain gate tells us He came from Heaven. The purple–color of royalty–reminds us that He is the King of kings. The scarlet is a reminder of the precious blood which flowed from His body when He died on the cross, a sacrifice for us. Have you come to God by this wonderful Door–the Saviour, Jesus Christ? (*Teacher:* Give clear invitation.)

Lesson 4
GOD'S WILLINGNESS TO BE WITH HIS PEOPLE

NOTE TO THE TEACHER

Throughout all of Scripture the mercy of God and His grace are intertwined. Mercy is God *not* giving us what we *do* deserve. Grace is God's giving us what we *do not* deserve. This is particularly evident in the study of Tabernacle truths.

God is so great, so mighty, that even the "heaven of heavens cannot contain Him." (See 2 Chronicles 2:6; 6:18; Psalm 139:7-12; Jeremiah 23:24.) Despite His majesty, the first house of God was a tent. His people, the Jews, were living in tents. So God, in His amazing love, planned a house for Himself like the houses of His people. He was willing to be among them in a tent!

In addition, He–the holy One–provided a way for sinful man to approach Him. Each sinner deserved the punishment of death. By God's mercy, he was spared. Through the grace of God, a substitute sacrifice took the sinner's place. Help your students to sense the awe of His love, His mercy, His grace.

In the first paragraph under illustration #15, we have this statement: "God accepted the blood of *animals* as a *covering* for the sins of those who offered them." We have not attempted to discuss this. But you should be informed, teacher, since your students may have questions.

Repeatedly in Exodus, Leviticus and Numbers, the word "atonement" appears. (See, for example, Exodus 30:10; 32:30; Leviticus 17:11.) It is a Hebrew word which means *to cover*. Each sacrifice that was offered covered the sin of the offerer and secured God's forgiveness. The punishment for sin was placed upon the animal (or bird) and the one who offered it was able to go free because his sins were covered. Sin can be covered and forgiven only through blood that is shed. But the blood of animals never *took away sins*. (See Hebrews 10:11.)

Cover the top part of illustration #17 until you speak of the word of God and the Lord Jesus.

Scripture to be studied: Exodus 27:1-8; 30:17-21; 38:1-8; Leviticus 3:7-8

The *aim* of the lesson: Forgiveness of sin is possible only through the shedding of blood.

What your students should *know*: That the Lamb of God takes away the sin of the world.

What your students should *feel*: A need for forgiveness and cleansing from sin.

What your students should *do*:
Unsaved: Receive Christ as Saviour from sin.
Saved: Receive cleansing through daily confession of sin.

Lesson outline for the teacher's and students' notebooks:
1. The brazen altar (Exodus 27:1-8; 38:1-7).
2. The offerings (Leviticus 3:7-8).
3. The Lord Jesus Christ, the Lamb of God (John 1:29).
4. The laver, the place of cleansing (Exodus 30:17-21; 38:8).

The verse to be memorized:
Unto Him who loved us and washed us from our sins in His own blood, (Revelation 1:5b)

THE LESSON

1. THE BRAZEN ALTAR
Exodus 27:1-8; 38:1-7

Phinehas walked slowly and thoughtfully toward the Tabernacle gate at the entrance to the court. The beautiful curtain hanging there was drawn aside. He could see a bronze altar inside the court.

Show Illustration #14

Eleazar, his father, explained, "Phinehas, that is the brazen altar. It is covered with bronze." (*Teacher:* In those days there was no brass. Though we we are used to the term "brazen altar" it was actually bronze.)

Phinehas had seen many altars. But all were made of stone or earth, not bronze. Altars, he knew, were used for sacrifices to God.

Eleazar continued, "God asks us to bring to Him animal sacrifices because of our sins. Sin must be punished. God could punish us for our sin. Instead, because of His grace and mercy, He allows an animal to die in place of the sinner." Phinehas thought he understood this.

Aaron, the grandfather of Phinehas, was standing by the altar. There were many things Phinehas wanted to know. He wondered why Grandfather Aaron was called the "high priest." He wondered about the splendid things his grandfather wore. He had many questions about the other priests who helped at the Tabernacle. Phinehas's father, Eleazar, knew the answers. For Eleazar was one of the priests (but not the high priest). However, these questions would have to wait. Right now Phinehas wanted to know more about the brazen altar.

His father explained, "There is wood underneath the bronze. It is acacia (shittim) wood–the wood of a small desert tree."

I want to tell *you* something which Phinehas did *not* know. Remember, the Tabernacle is a picture of the Lord Jesus Christ. The brazen altar was a furnishing in the Tabernacle court. It, too, is a picture of Christ. We know that the first man (Adam) was made from the dust of the earth. Hundreds of years later, the Lord Jesus left Heaven and came into this world as a man. The Bible speaks of Him as "a root out of a dry ground" (Isaiah 53:2). Does that remind you of a small desert (dry ground) tree? Do you see the picture?

Phinehas had seen the men working with the bronze. He knew it was a strong metal–hard and lasting. Its shape was not easily changed, even with the tools the metal workers used.

Just as the bronze is strong, so the Lord Jesus is strong. He does not change His mind about what is right and wrong. We are often changeable about sin. Because our friends think something wrong is right, we try to make ourselves believe it is right. The Lord Jesus is not like this. His feeling towards sin never changes. He always hates it!

The brazen altar was bigger than any altar Phinehas had ever seen. Eleazar explained, "The people who are rich bring to the Lord large sacrifices–cattle from their herds." Phinehas realized that a bull cut in pieces would cover the grate on the altar.

– 29 –

2. THE OFFERINGS
Leviticus 3:7-8

Even as he watched, a man brought a lamb to the gate of the Tabernacle where the priest met him. This man was not rich, nor was he a priest. If he had been, he would have brought a bull. He was not extremely poor, else he would have brought a dove. God had given exact instructions as to how various kinds of people should worship Him. (See Leviticus 4:3, 14, 24, 32; 5:7, 11-13.) By bringing his offering, the man was confessing that God is holy and must punish sin. He was admitting that he himself was a sinner. But the penalty for his sin would be paid by this substitute.

Show Illustration #15

Phinehas watched as the man put his hand on the head of the lamb, closed his eyes and prayed. Then the lamb–a perfect one–was slain. It had no broken leg, no sore eye, no wound in its flesh. For only the blood of a perfect animal would do as a covering for sin.

3. THE LORD JESUS CHRIST, THE LAMB OF GOD
John 1:29

Show Illustration #16

Here we have another wonderful picture of the Lord Jesus Christ. He is the Lamb of God. (See John 1:29.) He is the perfect One. (See 1 Peter 2:22-23.) When He died on the cross, blood flowed from His body. Why did He give His blood? (See John 10:17-18.) To take away sin. God accepted the blood of *animals* as a *covering* for the sins of those who offered them. (Read Psalm 32:1; 85:2.) Each sin required another sacrifice. But only the blood of the *Lord Jesus Christ* can *take away sin* and remove its penalty *forever.* (See John 1:29; Hebrews 10:11-14; Revelation 1:5.)

For hundreds of years, thousands of animals were sacrificed for the sins of the people. But when the Lord Jesus Christ died on the cross, He declared, "It is finished." Never again would any animal have to die for a sinner. (See Hebrews 9:25-28; 1 Peter 3:18.)

"Phinehas, my son, there is only one way we can worship God," his father explained. "That is to come through the gate and bring our sacrifice to be slain." (So it is with us. We cannot worship God unless we come through the blood of the Lord Jesus Christ who is our sacrifice for sin.)

Phinehas was glad to observe that the altar was not too high for a child to reach the top. (*Teacher:* Its height was approximately 4½ feet.) Children, too, can worship God.

Phinehas was eager to know about the other piece of furniture in the court. "Father, may I see what it's like?" he asked.

"You may look at it from here. Only the priests may go beyond the brazen altar, Phinehas. Because you are a grandson of Aaron, you are in the priestly family. This means that when you are grown, you will serve as a priest. Then you will go beyond the brazen altar." Phinehas felt his heart beat faster. It would be wonderful to serve God in such a way!

4. THE LAVER, THE PLACE OF CLEANSING
Exodus 30:17-21; 38:8

Eleazar continued, "The other piece of furniture in the court is the laver. It is the place of washing. We priests wash our hands and feet there when we are finished with our work at the altar." (See Exodus 30:18; 38:3; Leviticus 8:11.)

Show Illustration #17

Squinting his eyes, Phinehas exclaimed, "It is so bright and shining, it hurts my eyes!"

"Son, your mother and the other women brought shining brass mirrors as their offerings for the Tabernacle. The laver is made of their polished mirrors."

"No wonder it is bright," Phinehas decided. Then another question popped into his mind. "Is there water in the laver?" he asked.

"Yes, there is water in the laver," Eleazar answered. "We priests may not go inside the Tabernacle unless our hands and feet are washed in the water at the laver."

Would you like to see another picture here? The laver, made of the mirrors, shows us the Lord Jesus, the living Word of God. A mirror shows us ourselves as we are. When we look into the perfect life of the Lord Jesus, we see ourselves as sinners. We are not like He is. His perfect life shows up the sin in us.

The washing, too, is a picture. When we receive the Lord Jesus Christ, we are bathed all over–we are made clean from sin. (See Titus 3:5.) But things often come into our lives that are displeasing to God. These things need to be taken care of. We do not receive the Lord Jesus Christ as Saviour all over again. But we confess our sins and He cleanses us of them. (See Proverbs 28:13; 1 John 1:9.) You see, we had "our bath" when Christ "washed us from our sins in His own blood." Now we need only to have our hands and feet washed. Alas, if they are not cleansed, we cannot be useful for God.

How do we know what is wrong in our lives? By reading the Word of God. "How can a young man cleanse his way? By taking heed to Your Word . . .Your Word have I hidden in my heart, that I might not sin against You." (See Psalm 119:9, 11.) Phinehas had to wait until he was a man before he could use the laver. But here is a wonderful truth. Today, all who have been washed from their sins by trusting in Christ, are priests right now! (See 1 Peter 2:5, 9; Revelation 1:6; 5:10.) By looking into the mirror of God's Word with its record of the perfect life of Christ, we shall want to be clean.

If you have never received the Lord Jesus as your Saviour from sin, will you do that right now? If you are already a child of God but have unconfessed sin, will you tell God about it this moment? Name those things which are wrong. Tell Him you are sincerely sorry for those sins and ask His forgiveness.